ULTIMATE MANGA

HOW TO DRAW
DRAMATIC MANGA

Marc Powell and David Neal

PowerKiDS press

New York

WITH THANKS TO ODA, STEVE, AILIN, AND PAT

Published in 2016 by **The Rosen Publishing Group**
29 East 21st Street, New York, NY 10010

Text by Jack Hawkins
Edited by Jack Hawkins
Designed by Dynamo Ltd and Emma Randall
Cover design by Notion Design
Illustrations by Marc Powell and David Neal

Cataloging-in-Publication Data

Powell, Marc.
How to draw dramatic manga / by Marc Powell and David Neal.
p. cm. — (Ultimate manga)
Includes index.
ISBN 978-1-4994-1141-6 (pbk.)
ISBN 978-1-4994-1151-5 (6 pack)
ISBN 978-1-4994-1174-4 (library binding)
1. Comic books, strips, etc. — Japan — Technique — Juvenile literature.
2. Cartooning — Technique — Juvenile literature. 3. Comic strip characters
— Japan — Juvenile literature. I. Title.
NC1764.5.J3 P694 2016
741.5'1—d23

Manufactured in the United States of America
CPSIA Compliance Information: Batch WS15PK: For Further Information
contact Rosen Publishing, New York, New York at 1-800-237-9932

CONTENTS

HOW TO USE THIS BOOK

The drawings in this book have been built up in seven stages. Each stage uses lines of a different color so you can see the new layer clearly. Of course, you don't have to use different colors in your work. Use a pencil for the first four stages so you can get your drawing right before moving on to the inking and coloring stages.

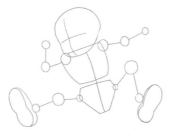

Stage 1: Green lines
This is the basic stick figure of your character.

Stage 2: Red lines
The next step is to flesh out the simple stick figure.

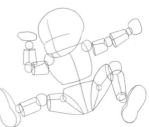

Stage 3: Blue lines
Then finish the basic shape and add in extra details.

Stage 4: Black lines
Add in clothes and any accessories.

Stage 5: Inks
The inking stage will give you a final line drawing.

Stage 6: Colors
"Flat" coloring uses lighter shades to set the base colors of your character.

Stage 7: Shading
Add shadows for light sources, and use darker colors to add depth to your character.

BASIC TOOLS

You don't need lots of complicated, expensive tools for your manga images – many of them are available from a good stationery shop. The others can be found in any art supplies store, or online.

PENCILS

These are probably the most important tool for any artist. It's important to find a type of pencil you are comfortable with, since you will be spending a lot of time using it.

Graphite

You will be accustomed to using graphite pencils – they are the familiar wood-encased "lead" pencils. They are available in a variety of densities from the softest, 9B, right up to the hardest, 9H. Hard pencils last longer and are less likely to smudge on the paper. Most artists use an HB (#2) pencil, which falls in the middle of the density scale.

Mechanical pencils

Also known as propelling pencils, these contain a length of lead that can be replaced. The leads are available in the same densities as graphite pencils. The great advantage of mechanical pencils over graphite is that you never have to sharpen them – you simply extend more lead as it wears down.

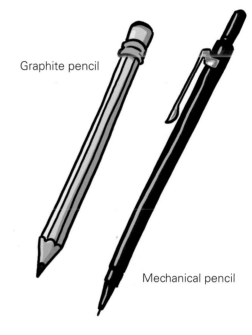

Graphite pencil

Mechanical pencil

Marker

Ballpoint pen

INKING PENS

After you have penciled your piece of artwork, you will need to ink the line to give a sharp, solid image.

Ballpoint pens

Standard ballpoint pens are ideal for lining your piece. However, their quality varies, as does their delivery of ink. A single good-quality ballpoint pen is better than a collection of cheap ones.

Marker pens

Standard marker pens of varying thicknesses are ideal for coloring and shading your artworks. They provide a steady, consistent supply of ink, and can be used to build layers of color by re-inking the same area. They are the tools most frequently used for manga coloring.

ROMANTIC HERO

Manga comics are full of dramatic situations. This handsome character might turn up in a romantic storyline. Will the female lead fall for him? Does he have a dark secret? There are so many different narrative possibilities.

STEP 1
Draw a tall stick figure with long legs. His right arm is extended towards the viewer, so his forearm is foreshortened.

STEP 2
Use cylinder shapes to give form to the character's arms and legs, then draw the lines marking the sides of his neck.

STEP 3

Draw the young man's basic anatomical details and facial features, then draw his hands. His right hand is holding a box of chocolates and the fingers of his left are curled inwards.

STEP 4

Give your character some hair, then add detail to his facial features. Draw his clothes and the bunch of flowers in his left hand. Add a bow to the box of chocolates.

STEP 5

Use your lining pen to go over
the lines that will be visible
in the finished drawing, and
erase any pencil lines.

STEP 6
Add in the shadows to show the creases in the man's clothes. The light source is coming from above and to his left.

STEP 7
Finish coloring the drawing.
The bright yellow of the
flowers and ribbon helps to
make the gifts stand out.

MYSTERIOUS OLD WOMAN

Here we have drawn a wise old lady. Her pose suggests she is rather frail, but her eyes twinkle with a sense of mischief. Does she know something she shouldn't? Is she tougher than she looks? Might she even have magical abilities?

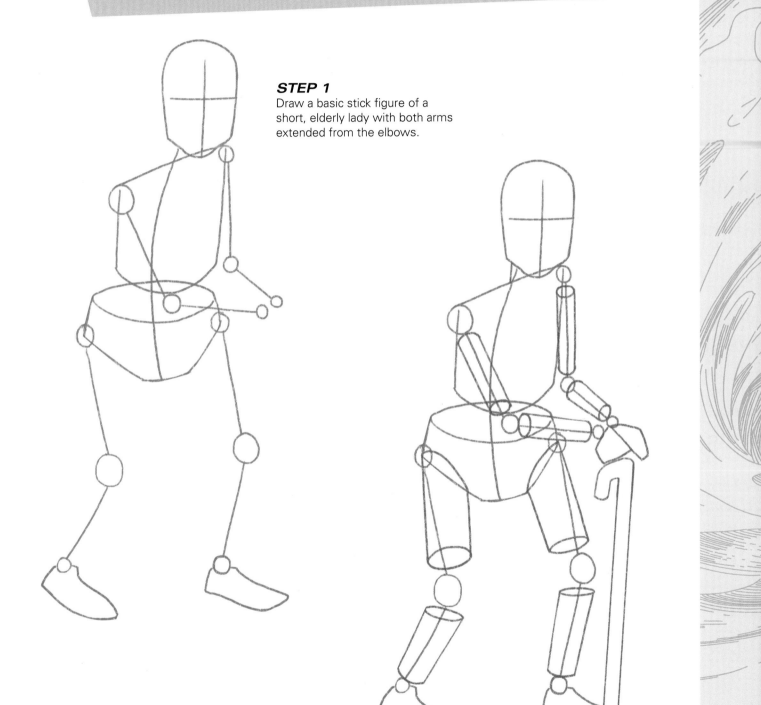

STEP 1
Draw a basic stick figure of a short, elderly lady with both arms extended from the elbows.

STEP 2
Use cylinder shapes to give form to the lady's arms and legs, then draw the line marking the side of her neck and the basic shapes of her hands, which are resting on the handle of a walking stick.

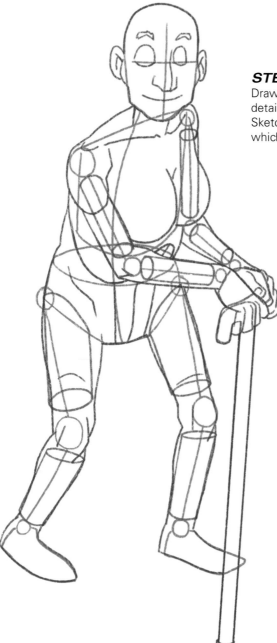

STEP 3

Draw your character's basic anatomical details – note that her body is quite stout. Sketch in her facial features and her fingers, which are wrapped around the stick.

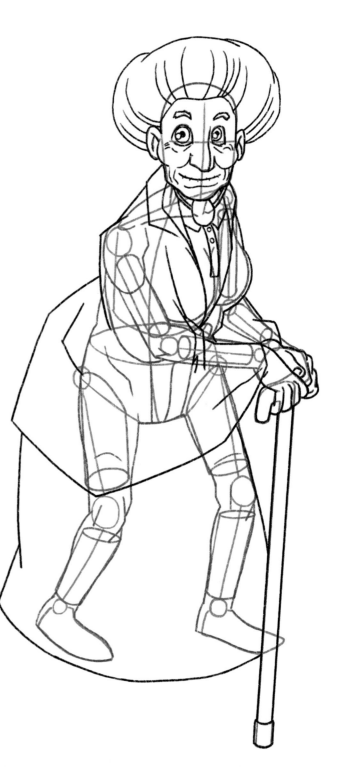

STEP 4

Give your character some hair and a blouse, a cape and a full-length skirt. Add details to her facial features and walking stick, then draw her necklace.

STEP 5

Use your lining pen to go over the lines that will be visible in the finished drawing, and erase any pencil lines. Put the finishing touches to her necklace.

STEP 6

We decided to use a single color for her cape and skirt, but you could shade her top half in a different tone to create the effect of a shawl.

STEP 7
Notice how the shadowing helps to define the flow of her arm beneath the material.

EXPRESSIONS

Almost any face can be transformed by some simple changes to eye and mouth shapes. Learning how to convey different emotions is a vital skill in your storytelling kit.

A simple way to practice is to draw a basic head shape a number of times. Look at yourself in the mirror as you make faces and note down the different shapes of your eyes, mouth, and so on. Then try out different combinations on your artwork to see how closely you can match your own expressions.

Here are some simple facial expressions to show you how to draw your characters so they display their emotions.

Anger
Angling the eyebrows down and narrowing the eyes will make your character look as if they are about to explode with anger. The mouth can be open or shown with a thin line.

Surprise
Raised, pointed eyebrows coupled with wide eyes and an open mouth shape make your character look like they have been caught off-guard by something.

Embarrassment
A slightly wide-eyed look and subtle shading across the nose and cheeks (use a pale red tint if you are adding color, to hint at blushing) show your character is feeling embarrassed.

Happiness
Narrowing the eyes and adding a wide smile gives the effect of the character's cheeks rising as part of the smile without you actually having to draw the cheeks.

Sadness
Tilting the head down and closing the eyes will show sadness, while adding streaks of tears down the face will really hammer the emotion home.

Goofy
A cheeky character may need a silly expression. One eye closed and the tongue popping out will give your character a goofy look.

Rage
A step up from anger, rage is expressed by more defined eyebrows and a much more open and angled mouth.

Fear
Wide-open eyes and large pupils, as well as a partly open mouth, illustrate fear.

Head shapes

A character's head shape can indicate a lot about his or her personality – for example, jovial shopkeepers can be happy and round-faced, while villains in manga tend to have more pointed, narrow faces.

There are four basic shapes to start with when drawing heads: ovals, squares, circles, and triangles. Experimenting with the different shapes can create some unique characters. Remember to bear in mind the character of your subject and try to lean towards using the traditional shape that's appropriate – though of course it's ultimately your artwork and if you want to create a character with a happy, round face who shocks everyone by being totally evil, that is up to you!

Triangular

Heads with sharp, pointed angles are good for villains. The sharp, angled style also lends itself well to drawing elves and other magical folk.

Oval

A lot of manga faces are based on the oval; it's a versatile shape for both male and female characters.

Circular

Comical characters are usually depicted with circular heads. The circular shape means you won't need a lot of definition in the face, but you'll need to concentrate on the eyes and mouth a lot more in order to convey the character effectively.

Square

Square, angled cheeks and chins and an overall square look to the head are useful for creating muscular, beefy, but not too smart henchmen.

KIMONO GIRL

This girl is created from smooth, curving lines, creating the impression that her personality is calm and gentle. This character offers excellent opportunities for you to practice drawing flowing hair and clothes.

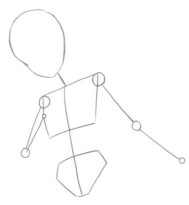

STEP 1

Draw a basic stick figure of a girl's torso, arms and head. Her legs will be hidden beneath a long skirt, so be sure to leave space on your paper for this. Her right forearm is bent upwards towards her shoulder.

STEP 2

Use cylinder shapes to give form to the girl's arms and draw two lines marking the sides of her neck, along with the basic shape of her left hand. Now draw the outline of her wide, floor-length skirt.

STEP 3
Draw the girl's basic anatomical details and facial features, then draw her hands. Her right hand is resting on her right collarbone and her left is scattering flowers. Now draw the folds at the bottom of her skirt.

STEP 4
Complete the girl's dress by adding long, flowing sleeves and a crossover bodice with a wide sash. Now draw her long, straight hair, which frames her face and fans out behind her back. Add details to her facial features and a few flowers just above her left ear.

STEP 5

Use your lining pen to go over the lines that will be visible in the finished drawing, and erase any pencil lines. Add petals to the flowers the girl is scattering and draw the bow shape behind her head.

STEP 6

Use darker colors to add shading and define the folds of her full skirt.

STEP 7
Color the flowers and the inside of her sleeve, then complete the coloring of your character using lighter shades as shown.

● **ARTIST'S TIP**
The swirl of the dress and the shading is a clever trick to draw the viewer's eyes up the dress and focus attention on the face of the character.

MAGICAL SHOPKEEPER

Not everyone in the world is six feet tall and devastatingly handsome. At first glance our shopkeeper might seem undistinguished but he's absolutely bursting with character, from his bushy mustache right down to his quirky little shoes.

STEP 1

Draw a short, stocky stick figure with his right arm raised from the elbow and his left arm bent, with the hand behind his back. Both feet are turned outwards.

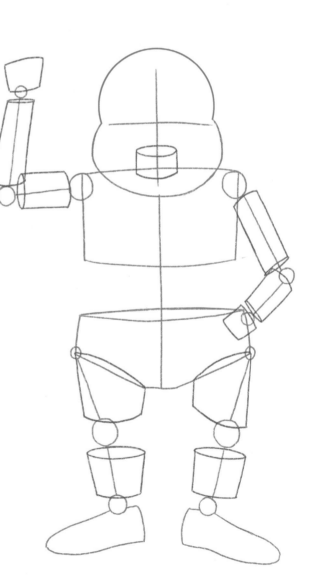

STEP 2

Use cylinder shapes to bulk out your character's arms and legs. His legs are short and wide. Draw a cylinder to mark the position of his neck, although this will be hidden behind his beard. Sketch in the basic shapes of his hands.

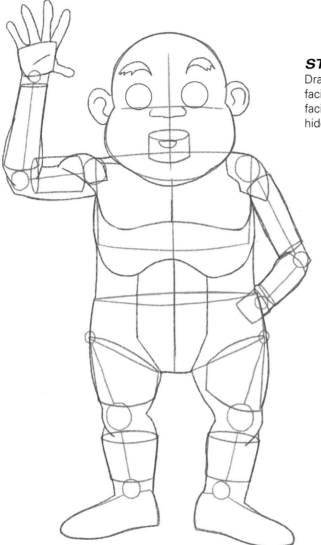

STEP 3

Draw your character's basic anatomical details and facial features. Draw his right hand with the palm facing forwards as if he is waving. His left hand is hidden behind his back.

STEP 4

Give your character a tuft of hair, a large mustache and a pointed beard. Complete his facial features and draw his clothes, including his apron and badge.

STEP 5

Use your lining pen to go over the lines that will be visible in the finished drawing, and erase any pencil lines. Add a couple of wrinkle lines above the shopkeeper's eyebrows.

STEP 6

Add the coloring using lighter shades as shown.

STEP 7

The light is coming from the shopkeeper's left-hand side. The curved shadowing on the front of the apron makes the character's stomach look round and chubby, giving him a friendly appearance.

DRAWING HAIR

There are so many ways of drawing hair that they could take up a whole book on their own. You can just do basic shapes and add simple lines to define the flow of the hair, as you will see in many of the illustrations in this book, or you can draw more elaborate hair which will really add to your character.

Manga hair can be very complex, but you can break it down into basic shapes to make it easier to draw. These shapes can vary in size, shape and thickness; they are often thicker at the top and curve at the bottom to create depth and volume.

You can combine these basic shapes to arrive at something that more closely resembles hair. The more strands you add, the more detailed the hair becomes.

The hair can be long and flowing or short and spiky.

Strands of hair naturally overlap and twist across one another. This helps with the illusion of movement in your drawing and gives it a three-dimensional feel. Make your hairstyles interesting by creating lots of twists and curls.

If you are depicting a character in dynamic motion, draw the lines of the hair in the direction of movement.

Here is a simple, neat way to create a finishing edge to hair if you don't want spikes or curls.

GUARDIAN ANGEL

An angel can be used very effectively to add a twist to your stories. Perhaps she sends your characters on a quest, or maybe she will help them escape from danger. The wings on this angel are tricky to get right, but the end result is worth the effort.

STEP 1

Draw a tall, slim stick figure with wide, feathery wing shapes extending from her shoulders. She has a feminine, pointed chin and her feet are hanging down because she is flying.

STEP 2

Use cylinder shapes to give form to the figure's slender arms and legs, then draw the lines marking the sides of her long neck and the basic shapes for her hands. Sketch in the train of her dress, which is floating down behind her legs.

STEP 3
Draw her basic anatomical details and facial features, including her wide, rounded eyes. Complete the drawing of her hands and wings.

STEP 4
Give the angel long, flowing hair, then add detail to her facial features, feet and wings. Draw her dress and mark the creases where it wraps and falls around her body.

STEP 5
Use your lining pen to go over the lines that will be visible in the finished drawing, and erase any pencil lines.

STEP 6
Put in the coloring of your character as shown. Pastel shades give her an ethereal appearance.

STEP 7
Use color to add shading and give depth to the folds of the angel's dress.

ARTIST'S TIP
An unbalanced artwork can look jarring to the eye. Notice in this image how the wings are equally sized on each side of the figure, with the arms balancing them out in a complementary pose. The hair curling over the shoulder is mirrored by the dress billowing out further down, leading to a well-balanced image.

GLOSSARY

beefy Muscular and tough.

bodice The part of a dress above the waist.

cape A short, sleeveless coat.

cheeky Slightly rude in an amusing way.

elaborate Complicated and intricate, having been created with great attention to detail.

ethereal Delicate in a way that appears to be from another world.

foreshortened Drawn shorter than it really is so that a picture appears to have depth.

frail Weak and easily hurt.

jarring Unexpected in a shocking way.

pastel A soft, delicate color.

quirky Unusual or unexpected.

sash A strip of cloth worn around the waist or over one shoulder.

scenario A setting for a story.

shawl A piece of fabric that is worn wrapped around the shoulders.

train A long piece of material at the back of a dress which trails along the floor.

FURTHER READING

Draw Your Own Manga: All the Basics by Haruno Nagatomo (Kodansha America, Inc, 2014)

Manga Now!: How to Draw Action Figures by Keith Sparrow (Search Press Ltd, 2014)

Write and Draw Your Own Comics by Louie Stowell (Usborne, 2014)

WEBSITES

Due to the changing nature of Internet links, PowerKids Press has developed an online list of websites related to the subject of this book. This site is updated regularly. Please use this link to access the list: **www.powerkidslinks.com/um/drama**

INDEX